Note to parents

All these songs have familiar pop tunes, so children will love to dance to them. There are also suggestions for ways to turn them into enjoyable games.

Acknowledgements

'Agadoo' © 1985 Les Editions Marouani.
Warner Chappell Music Ltd., London W1Y 3FA.
By M. Symile, M. Delancery and J. Peram.
Used by permission.

'Simple Simon says' written and composed by Storman/Jacobson.
Copyright Control.

'The Locomotion' by Gerry Goffin and Carole King
© 1962 Screen Gems–EMI Music Inc. USA.
Screen Gems–EMI Music Ltd., London EC2H 0EA.
Used by permission.

'Superman' written and composed by
Famonetti/Cecchetto. Copyright Control.

'D.I.S.C.O.' written and composed by
Jean Kluger and Daniel Vangarde.
© 1979 Editions Bleu Blanc Rouge/Editions et Productions Zagora.
Chelsea Music Publishing Co. Ltd. (for the UK and Eire).

'I should be so lucky' written and composed by Stock/Aitken/Waterman
© 1987 All Boys Music Ltd.

Every effort has been made to trace the owner(s) of the copyright of these songs. We offer our sincere apologies if we have used copyright material without due acknowledgement.

Party Pops

Illustrated by Sarah Hedley

Copyright © 1992 World International Publishing Limited and
Cassettes for Young People Limited.
All rights reserved.
Published in Great Britain by World International Publishing Limited,
an Egmont Company, Egmont House, PO Box 111, Great Ducie Street,
Manchester M60 3BL.

Printed in Germany. ISBN 0 7498 0956 6

A catalogue record for this book is available from the British Library

Agadoo

Chorus:

Agadoo doo doo, push pineapple,
shake the tree,

*Make a pushing movement,
and then clasp your hands and wiggle them.*

Agadoo doo doo, push pineapple,
grind coffee,

*Make a pushing movement,
and twirl your hands round and round each other.*

To the left, to the right, jump up and down
and to the knees,

*Wave your hands to the left, then to the right,
then jump up and down and touch your knees.*

Come and dance every night,
sing with a hula melody.

I met a hula mistress somewhere in Waikiki,
Well, she was selling pineapple, playing ukelele,
And when I went to the girl,
    "Come on and teach me to sway,"
She laughed and whispered to me,
    "Yes, come tonight to the bay."

The lovely beach and the sky,
    the moon of Kauai,
The rum calypso sarong,
    well, I'll be singing this song.

Repeat chorus twice.

Down on the shore,
    they gathered romance,
She showed me much more,
    not only to dance.

Repeat chorus twice.

Simple Simon says

Do what the words tell you.

I'd like to play a game that is so much fun,
And it's not so very hard to do.
The name of the game is 'Simple Simon says',
And I would like for you to play it too.

Put your hands in the air
(Simple Simon says),

Shake them all about
(Simple Simon says),

Do it when Simon says
(Simple Simon says),
And you will never be out.

Simple Simon says put your hands on your hips,
Let your backbone slip, Simon says.
Simple Simon says put your hands on your hips,
Let your backbone slip, Simon says.

Put your hands on your head
(Simple Simon says),

Bring them down by your side
(Simple Simon says),

Shake them to your left
(Simple Simon says),
And shake them to your right.

Repeat last verse

Now that you have learnt to play
    this game with me,
You can see it's not so hard to do.
Try it once again, this time more carefully,
And I hope the winner will be you.

    Clap your hands in the air
    (Simple Simon says),

    Do it double time
    (Simple Simon says),

    Slow it down like before
    (Simple Simon says),
    Now you're looking fine.

Repeat last verse

Well, shake your hands in the air
(Simple Simon says),

Shake them all about
(Simple Simon says),

Do it when Simon says
(Simple Simon says),
And you will never be out.

The Locomotion

Everybody's doing a brand new dance now

*Put your arms out in front of you (first right, then left)
with palms down, then turn your palms
(first right, then left) to face up.*

Come on, baby...

*Put your right hand on your left arm,
then your left hand on your right arm.*

...do the locomotion,

*Jump back and forward again quickly turning
to face the right as you do it.
Swing your arms back by your sides
like train pistons as you turn.*

Repeat the actions throughout the verses.

I know you'll get to like it if you give it a chance now
(Come on, baby, do the locomotion),
My little baby sister can do it with ease,
It's easier than learning your ABC,
So come on, come on, do the locomotion with me.

Do what the words tell you.

Chorus:
>You've got to swing your hips now,
>Come on, baby, jump up, jump back,
>Well, I think you've got the knack, oh oh oh.

*Line up one behind the other like a train
and repeat all the actions.*

Now that you can do it, let's make a chain now
>(Come on, baby, do the locomotion),
A chugga chugga motion like a railway train now
>(Come on, baby, do the locomotion),
Do it nice and easy, now don't lose control,
A little bit of rhythm and a lot of soul,
So come on, come on, do the locomotion with me.

Second chorus:
The locomotion, come on, come on,
    the locomotion,
Come on, come on, the locomotion,
Come on, come on, come on, come on.

Move around the floor in a loco-motion
    (Come on, baby, do the locomotion),
Do it holding hands, if you get the notion
    (Come on, baby, do the locomotion),
There's never been a dance that's so easy to do,
It even makes you happy when you're feeling blue,
So come on, come on, do the locomotion with me.

Repeat chorus

Repeat second verse

Repeat second chorus

Superman

Do what the words tell you.

One two, one two three, go!
Clap your hands, sleep,

Wave your hands, hitch a ride,

Sneeze, go for a walk,

Let's see you swim, now ski,

Spray, macho man,

Sound your horn, ring the bell,

Okay, kiss, comb your hair,

Wave your hands, come on, wave your hands,

Superman! Ohhhhh!

Repeat

>*Do the actions as quickly as you can!*

(Fast)
Sleep, wave, hitch a ride, sneeze, walk, swim,
Ski, spray, macho, blow your horn, ring the bell,
Okay, kiss, comb your hair, wave, c'mon,
      give 'em a wave,
Superman! Ohhhhhh!

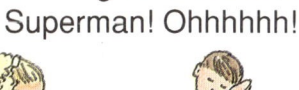

D.I.S.C.O.

Once you know the words, you can divide into two teams. One team sings the words in brackets, and the other team sings the other words.

Chorus:
(D.I.S.C.O.)
(D.I.S.C.O.)
(D.I.S.C.O.)
(D.I.S.C.O.)
She is disco (D.I.S.C.O.),
She is disco (D.I.S.C.O.),
She is disco (D.I.S.C.O.),
She is disco (D.I.S.C.O.),

She is D (Delirious),
She is I (Incredible),
She is S (Superficial),
She is C (Complicated),
She is Oh Oh Oh.
She is D (Desirable),
She is I (Irresistible),
She is S (Super sexy),
She is C (Such a cutie),
She is Oh Oh Oh.

Repeat chorus

She is D (Disastrous),
She is I (Impossible),
She is S (Super special),
She is C (Crazy, crazy),
She is Oh Oh Oh.
She is D (Delightful),
She is I (Incredible),
She is S (Sensational),
She is C (Sweet as candy),
She is Oh Oh Oh.

Repeat chorus
Repeat first verse
Repeat chorus

I should be so lucky

In my imagination,
> there is no complication,

I dream about you all the time,
In my mind a celebration,
> the sweetest love sensation,

Thinking you could be mine.
In my imagination,
> there is no hesitation,

We walk together hand in hand, I'm dreaming,
You fell in love with me,
> like I'm in love with you,

But dreaming's all I do,
> if only they'd come true.

Chorus

I should be so lucky, lucky, lucky, lucky,
I should be so lucky in love.
I should be so lucky, lucky, lucky, lucky,
I should be so lucky in love.

It's a crazy situation,
> you always keep me waiting,

Because it's only make believe.
And I would come a-running,
> to give you all my loving,

If one day you would notice me.
My heart is close to breaking,
> and I can't go on faking

The fantasy that you'll be mine, I'm dreaming
That you're in love with me,
> like I'm in love with you,

But dreaming's all I do,
> if only they'd come true.

Repeat chorus

Repeat first verse

Repeat chorus